PHONIC PICTURES

INITIAL SOUNDS AND BLENDS

Written by
Jane Beals

Published by
World Teachers Press®

Published with the permission of R.I.C. Publications Pty. Ltd.

First published by R.I.C. Publications Pty. Ltd., Perth, Western Australia. Revised by Didax Educational Resources.

Printed in the United States of America.

Order Number 2-5181
ISBN 1-58324-115-9

D E F G H I 07 06 05 04 03

Educational Resources
395 Main Street
Rowley, MA 01969
www.worldteacherspress.com

Phonic Pictures

Foreword

Phonic Pictures, the fourth book in the *Phonics in Action* series, contains full-page pictures of initial sounds, blends and digraphs. Students are required to view the scene and identify pictures of objects or actions beginning with the phonic sound presented.

A list of possible answers is included, though students may interpret other suggestions.

The reproducible pages are best used as a whole-class or small-group activity. However, each can be used as a one-on-one confidence building experience for the less able or more immature early reader.

Contents

Teachers Notes

Possible answers that can be identified in each picture are included on pages 55–56. Students may interpret suggestions other than those listed. In the case of initial vowel sounds, items that contain the vowel sound have also been included. Some initial letters and blends have been combined due to the difficulty in the amount of items that can be illustrated for the particular sound.

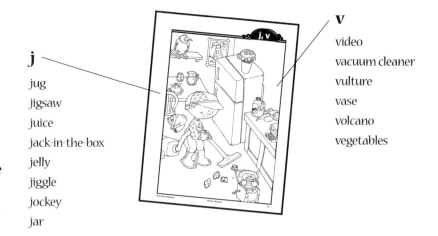

j

jug
jigsaw
juice
jack-in-the-box
jelly
jiggle
jockey
jar

v

video
vacuum cleaner
vulture
vase
volcano
vegetables

Suggestions for using the reproducible pages.

1.   Laminate for durability, marking, or labeling pictures in semi-permanent felt pen.

2.   As a group, or individually, students scan the picture and list, circle, or color items beginning with the sound being presented.

3.   Use as a group or individual reading game. Students use counters to cover pictures—in rotation if a group activity.

4.   Use as a teacher-directed activity. Students call out items in rotation and you list the actual words. These can be used in sight vocabulary and spelling lists.

5.   Associate as a "sound of the week" or "day" promotion. Students bring along items from home or cut pictures from magazines to add to a class display, along with the particular phonic picture.

6.   Use as a one-on-one activity to introduce or reinforce a particular phonic sound with less able or more immature early readers.

Also in the Phonics in Action series:

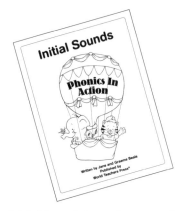

Initial Sounds introduces each letter of the alphabet.

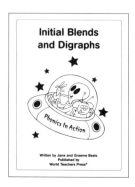

Initial Blends and Digraphs introduces initial blends and digraphs.

Final Consonant Sounds introduces single final consonant sounds and final blends and digraphs.

Phonic Pictures – Phonics in Action

Phonic Pictures – Phonics in Action

CEMENT

CE

Phonic Pictures – Phonics in Action

Phonic Pictures – Phonics in Action

g

h

Phonic Pictures – Phonics in Action

Phonic Pictures – Phonics in Action

Phonic Pictures – Phonics in Action

k

Phonic Pictures – Phonics in Action ©*World Teachers Press*®

milk
milk

talent show

Phonic Pictures – Phonics in Action

Phonic Pictures – Phonics in Action

Phonic Pictures – Phonics in Action

Phonic Pictures – Phonics in Action

Phonic Pictures – Phonics in Action

UP

1.

2.

DOWN

3.

5.

Phonic Pictures – Phonics in Action

dr

Phonic Pictures – Phonics in Action

Phonic Pictures – Phonics in Action ©World Teachers Press®

Phonic Pictures – Phonics in Action

Phonic Pictures – Phonics in Action ©World Teachers Press®

Phonic Pictures – Phonics in Action

Phonic Pictures – Phonics in Action

Phonic Pictures – Phonics in Action

pl

Phonic Pictures – Phonics in Action

Phonic Pictures – Phonics in Action

sk

Phonic Pictures – Phonics in Action

Phonic Pictures – Phonics in Action

Phonic Pictures – Phonics in Action

Phonic Pictures – Phonics in Action

str

Phonic Pictures – Phonics in Action

Phonic Pictures – Phonics in Action

ch

SHA
2.00

Phonic Pictures – Phonics in Action

Phonic Pictures – Phonics in Action

Answers

Initial letters

(initial blends are not included)

Page 5 – a

(Short) astronaut, apple, animals, acrobat, adventurous, altitude, ankle – hat, hanger, hand (Long) angel – plane, lake, gate, halo, tail, sail (Other) airport, flight attendant

Page 6 – b

balloon, boy, bird, butterfly, boat, bug, beetle, beach, ball, baby, boots, belt, beads, button, belly, basket, bun, book, beard, bib, bark, buckle, bounce

Page 7 – c

(Hard) cord, cushions, construction, castle, cocoon, carrot, cauliflower, cat, computer, calendar, calculator, camera, cactus, caterpillar, cupboard, cup, corner (Soft) celery, cereal, cement, cylinder, circus tent, ceiling

Page 8 – d

dog, duck, deer, dinosaur, daisy, dandelion, daffodil, doughnut, doll, dots, door, deck

Page 9 – e

(Short) elephant, egg – leg, peg, head (Long) eagle, easel, earring, emu, eel – feet, tree, knee (Other) eye

Page 10 – f

fire, fish, fireman, firetruck, fairy, finger, fence, fishbowl, fire hose, face

Page 11 – g

(Soft) giraffe, giant (Hard) gate, garden, goat, goose, geese, girl

Page 12 – h

helicopter, hay, hammer, hand, handyman, house, hedgehog, horse, hedge, hen, handle, hat, hair, hills

Page 13 – i

(Short) insect, ink, igloo, Innuit – bricks, lip, chin, fin, flippers, grin, slip, lick (Long) iron, ice cream, ice, icy, icicles – glide, slide

Page 14 – j and v

jug, jigsaw, juice, jack-in-the-box, jiggle, jockey, jar, video, vacuum cleaner, vulture, vase, volcano, vegetables

Page 15 – k

kiss, kiwi, kangaroo, koala, kilt, key, kitten, kick, kite, kid

Page 16 – l

lilies, life jacket, lifeboat, letter, laughing, land, log, line, lobster, Lucy, life saver, leaf

Page 17 – m

milk truck, microwave, mandolin, mountain, mouse, motorcycle, map, mermaids, music, mirror, man, mudflap

Page 18 – n

nest, newspaper, necklace, navy, net, nut, nine, notice, needle, nail, nanny

Page 19 – o

(Short) orange, octopus, otter, office building, omelette (Long) open – bow, nose, window, elbow (Other) onion, owl, oven

Page 20 – p

peach, pear, pineapple, pirate, pies, pencil, painter, paintbrush, paint, pen, paper, patch, panda, parrot, polka dots, poster

Page 21 – q and x

queen, quilt, quiet, quiver, quack, x-ray

Page 22 – r

rabbit, radio, rose, rainbow, rooster, rat, racquet, rocket, rink, river, rocks, rollerskates

Page 23 – s

seagull, sun, sail, surf, surfer, surfboard, sink, sandcastle, seahorse, seaweed, sea star, sandal, sausage, sand, seal, sandwich, seashore

Page 24 – t

Tyrannosaurus Rex, tank, tent, tent peg, ties, tin cans, towel, tired, tummy, tail, tassels

Page 25 – u

(Short) under, umbrella, up, undercover, shrub, thumb, button (Long) ukulele, uniform, unicorn, Uranus

Page 26 – w

witch, windmill, web, witch's hat, watch, wand, water, window

Page 27 – y

yin, yang, yo-yo, yolk, yak

Page 28 – z

zoo, zebra, zig-zag, zipper, zebra crossing, zero, zeppelin

Answers

Initial blends and digraphs

(single initial sounds are not included)

Page 29 - br

bridle, bridge, bride, bridegroom, bran, broom, brush, broccoli, brooch, break, bricks, brother, bread, breadcrumbs

Page 30 - cr

cry, crocodile, crab, crayfish, craters, crane, crown, crowd, crutch, crossword puzzle, crayon

Page 31 - dr

dragonfly, dragon, dribble, drum, drive, driver, dream, dress, dresser, drawers

Page32 - fr

fright, frying pan, fried egg, frog, fruit, fridge, freezer, frame, freckles

Page 33- gr

grandstand, grandfather, grandmother, grasshopper, grass, ground, grapefruit

Page 34- pr

present, princess, propeller

Page 35- tr

train, tree, tracks, trolley, tractor, tray, trowel, triangle, travel, truck

Page 36 - bl

blocks, (Mrs.) Black, blow, blindfold, blossoms, Blind Man's Bluff, blue, blouse, blink

Page 37 - cl

clown, clarinet, clock, cloth, clap, clamp, cloak, cliff, clouds, climb, clever, clothes

Page 38 - fl

flamingo, flame, flies, float, flag, flood, flowers, flute, flap

Page 39 - gl

globe, glove, glider, glasshouse, glow-worm, glasses, glass, glaciers, glad, gliding, glow, glee

Page 40 - pl

plug, platypus, plate, plant, planet, plane, plow, playground, playing

Page 41 - sl

sled, slide, slip, sleep, slug, sleeping bag, slippery, slippers

Page 42 - sc and sw

scorpion, scarecrow, scarf, scales, scar, swing, swan, swim, swimmer, swallows, swimming

Page 43 - sk

skip, skipping rope, skunk, ski, sky, skates, skyscraper, skateboard

Page 44 - sn and sm

snail, snake, snowman, snow, snorkel, snorkeling, sneeze, snowflake, smoke, smile, small

Page 45 - sp

spade, spaghetti, spinning wheel, space dog, spider, spear, spoon, spaceman, spaceship, spindle, (outer) space

Page 46 - st

stairs, stilts, stethoscope, star, stingray, starfish, statue, stamp, stool, stick, stapler, stag, staircase, stump

Page 47 - scr and spr

scratch, screw, scribble, screwdriver, screen, scroll, spring, spray, sprout, sprinkle, sprinkler

Page 48 - spl, squ and shr

splash, splinter, splatter, squirrel, squash, squid, squabble, squeeze, squish, shrimp, shrub, shrug

Page 49 - str

street, stroke, stripes, stream, stroller, straw hat, stretcher, stroll, strong, stretch, string, strap

Page 50 - tw and thr

twist, twirl, twinkle, twig, twelve, tweezers, twins, throw, throne, thread, threadbare, three, throat

Page 51 - ch

cheetah, cherries, chase, chain, chop, chair, chisel, cheese, chess, chopsticks, chicken, chimpanzee, cheeky, church, checkered, children

Page 52 - sh

shop, shampoo, shaggy, shoes, shed, shovel, shakes, shelves, ship, shipwreck, shower, shark, shoulder, shoelace, shawl, shirt, shorts, shin

Page 53 - th

thermometer, thumb, thump, thermos, think, thigh, thirsty

Page 54 - wh

whale, whirlpool, whip, wheelbarrow, whistle, wharf, wheel, white